THE PRINCIPLES OF DEMOCRACY

WHAT IS RESPECT?

 JOSHUA TURNER

New York

Published in 2020 by The Rosen Publishing Group, Inc.
29 East 21st Street, New York, NY 10010

Copyright © 2020 by The Rosen Publishing Group, Inc.

All rights reserved. No part of this book may be reproduced in any form without permission in writing from the publisher, except by a reviewer.

First Edition

Editor: Melissa Raé Shofner
Book Design: Reann Nye

Photo Credits: Seriest art Bplanet/Shutterstock.com; cover Monkey Business Images/Shutterstock.com; p. 5 metamorworks/Shutterstock.com; p. 7 andresr/E+/Getty Images; p. 9 Joseph Scherschel/The LIFE Picture Collection/Getty Images; p. 11 https://commons.wikimedia.org/wiki/File:JamesMadison.jpg; p. 13 Pressmaster/Shutterstock.com; p. 15 AFP/Getty Images; p. 17 John Roman Images/Shutterstock.com; p. 19 Alistair Berg/DigitalVision/Getty Images; p. 21 EMMANUEL DUNAND/AFP/Getty Images; p. 22 Rawpixel.com/Shutterstock.com.

Cataloging-in-Publication Data

Names: Turner, Joshua.
Title: What is respect? / Joshua Turner.
Description: New York : PowerKids Press, 2020. | Series: The principles of democracy | Includes glossary and index.
Identifiers: ISBN 9781538342848 (pbk.) | ISBN 9781538342862 (library bound) | ISBN 9781538342855 (6 pack)
Subjects: LCSH: Civil society–United States–Juvenile literature. | Toleration–United States–Juvenile literature. | Respect–Juvenile literature. | Freedom of expression–United States–Juvenile literature. | Democracy–United States–Juvenile literature.
Classification: LCC JK1759.T87 2019 | DDC 300.973–dc23

Manufactured in the United States of America

CPSIA Compliance Information: Batch #CSPK19: For Further Information contact Rosen Publishing, New York, New York at 1-800-237-9932

CONTENTS

★★★★★★★★★★★★

WHAT IS RESPECT? 4

THE GOLDEN RULE 6

RESPECT AND DEMOCRACY 8

FREEDOM OF SPEECH 10

RESPECT AND FAIRNESS. 12

DOES EVERYONE
    DESERVE RESPECT? 14

RESPECTING AUTHORITY 16

WAYS TO SHOW RESPECT 18

AGREEABLE DISAGREEMENT 20

NO RESPECT, NO DEMOCRACY 22

GLOSSARY 23

INDEX .24

WEBSITES 24

WHAT IS RESPECT?

Respect is the understanding that every person is worthwhile and that ideas should be shared and talked about **seriously**. Respect is also the understanding that everyone is good at something and has a part to play in society.

Respect can be earned through good actions, high-quality work, or from being skilled at a certain task. Respect is something that everyone wants, but it can be hard to earn. Respected members of society are often hardworking, caring, and trustworthy people who give back to their communities.

THE SPIRIT OF DEMOCRACY

Martin Luther King Jr. was a respected civil-rights **activist**—not just because of what he did, but how he did it. King didn't like **violence**. Instead, he used peaceful **protests** to bring about change.

People who work hard are often respected members of their community.

5

THE GOLDEN RULE

The golden rule is the idea that you should always treat others the way you want to be treated. This means if you want others to treat you with respect, you'll have to respect others. Looking down on others or being disrespectful means others will look down on and not think well of you.

Lack of respect in a society means more than just not being liked. It could also have an effect on your work, your ideas, or even your ability to make new friends.

Treating others the way you would want to be treated leads to better outcomes for everyone.

RESPECT AND DEMOCRACY

In a democracy, each person gets a vote and a voice in government. Respect is important because people will often disagree. Ideas about government and laws are very important to people. If we don't respect each other's ideas, it can lead to problems.

Even though everyone has a say in a democracy, people won't always get their way. It's important to respect all sides of an argument, even the losing side. Think of the golden rule, and remember you might not always be on the winning side.

THE SPIRIT OF DEMOCRACY

John Adams was the first president to lose a reelection campaign. Still, he had great respect for the United States, the office of president, and the people who voted for his **opponent**, Thomas Jefferson.

Richard Nixon and John F. Kennedy took part in the first televised presidential **debate**. Both men showed respect for each other and the voters.

FREEDOM OF SPEECH

Freedom of speech means that all people have the right to voice their opinions without fear of being **censored**. This right is the First **Amendment** of the U.S. Constitution, and it's based on the idea of respect for others.

Other people might say things you disagree with, but in a democracy, this is their right. There are limits on free speech, though. Speech meant to **encourage** violence or that puts peoples lives in danger is not **protected** by the Constitution.

> James Madison was the author of the Bill of Rights, which is the part of the Constitution that contains the First Amendment.

RESPECT AND FAIRNESS

Fairness in a democracy means giving every person a chance to reach their goals or voice their opinions regardless of their **gender**, social class, or **ethnicity**. Respect is an important part of treating others fairly.

If you don't respect a person's background or the work they bring to society, it becomes harder to treat them in a fair manner. When you have respect for someone and their point of view, treating them fairly is much easier. This is good for society.

THE SPIRIT OF DEMOCRACY

One of the reasons workers' rights movements have been successful in the United States is because the workers' contributions to society have been respected.

Treating others with respect makes them more likely to treat you with respect.

DOES EVERYONE DESERVE RESPECT?

If respect is good for society, should every person be treated with respect no matter what? Respect is given to others, but it must be earned through good actions and deeds.

If a person behaves in ways that harm or put down others, they may not be worthy of the respect of others. However, it's important to give people the benefit of the doubt. This means that until you know for sure what someone is like, you need to **assume** they mean well.

It's important to understand both sides of an argument before you judge someone and decide not to treat them with respect.

14

15

RESPECTING AUTHORITY

There are lots of different authority figures people meet in their lifetimes. Parents, elders, police officers, teachers, bosses, and government workers are all authority figures at some point in our lives.

Having respect for authority figures doesn't mean you'll always agree with them, but it does mean taking what they say seriously. A person might disagree with the president, but they should respect his or her authority because they were elected by a majority of people. In a democracy, the will of the majority is respected.

THE SPIRIT OF DEMOCRACY

When people running for a government office lose an election, they often wish their opponent well. This is how we show respect to the **process** of elections and the will of the majority.

Society respects authority figures such as police officers because they put their lives on the line to serve and protect others.

WAYS TO SHOW RESPECT

There are many ways to show respect for others in society. Saying "thank you" to someone when they do something for you, listening carefully to an opinion you disagree with, or being quiet while someone else is talking are all ways you can show respect to someone.

Having respect doesn't always mean you have to do something. It could also mean not doing something. For example, it's respectful to not yell at someone, even if they say something that makes you mad.

There are lots of ways to show respect, even when people are on opposing teams.

AGREEABLE DISAGREEMENT

An important part of respect is being able to disagree with someone without being mean or rude in response. Calling people names or yelling at them is not good for democracy.

Anyone could have something valuable to add to society. But if we're mean and only argue over disagreements, we might miss ideas that could be helpful. Having respect for people expressing different points of view makes the sharing of ideas much more fun and valuable.

THE SPIRIT OF DEMOCRACY

When John McCain ran for president in 2008, he made sure to tell his supporters that Barack Obama was a good person, even though the two men disagreed on important issues.

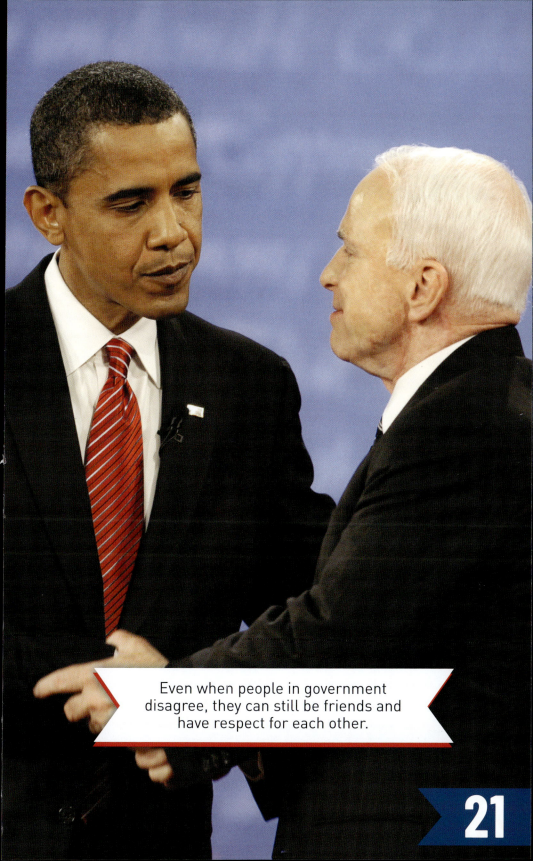

Even when people in government disagree, they can still be friends and have respect for each other.

21

NO RESPECT, NO DEMOCRACY

For a democracy to work, people need to respect each other, even when they don't see eye to eye. People in democratic societies settle their disagreements by talking out their problems and sharing their ideas.

In a democracy, we recognize that everyone has value and that everyone's ideas should be taken into account when making decisions. We might not always agree with what someone else has to say, but they have a right to say it, and it's important to respect that right.

GLOSSARY

★ ★ ★ ★ ★ ★ ★ ★ ★ ★ ★

activist: Someone who acts strongly in support of or against an issue.

amendment: A change in the words or meaning of a law or document, such as a constitution.

assume: To think that something is true or probably true without knowing that it is true.

censor: To remove things that are thought to be harmful to society.

debate: A discussion in which people share different opinions about something.

encourage: To try to win over to a cause or action.

ethnicity: Of or relating to large groups of people who have the same customs, religion, and origin.

gender: Relating to a person being male or female.

opponent: A person, team, or group that is competing against another in a contest.

process: A series of actions that produce something or that lead to a particular result.

protect: To keep safe.

protest: To show strong disapproval of something at a public event with other people.

serious: Dealing with matters in a thoughtful way; not trying to be funny.

violence: Using force to harm someone.

23

INDEX

A
authority figures, 16

B
benefit of the doubt, 14

C
Constitution, 10

F
fairness, 12
First Amendment, 10
freedom of speech, 10

G
golden rule, 6, 8

L
laws, 8

M
majority, 16

P
points of view, 12, 20

V
violence, 10
vote, 8

WEBSITES

Due to the changing nature of Internet links, PowerKids Press has developed an online list of websites related to the subject of this book. This site is updated regularly. Please use this link to access the list: www.powerkidslinks.com/pofd/resp